THE BATTLE OF BRITAIN

Neil R. Storey

SHIRE PUBLICATIONS

Published in Great Britain in 2012 by Shire Publications Ltd,
Midland House, West Way, Botley, Oxford OX2 0PH,
United Kingdom.

44-02 23rd Street, Suite 219, Long Island City,
NY 11101, USA.

E-mail: shire@shirebooks.co.uk   www.shirebooks.co.uk

© 2012 Neil Storey

A CIP catalogue record for this book is available from the
British Library.

Shire Library no. 644   .   ISBN-13: 978 0 74781 047 6

Neil Storey has asserted his right under the Copyright,
Designs and Patents Act, 1988, to be identified as the
author of this book.

Designed by Myriam Bell Design, UK and typeset
in Perpetua and Gill Sans.
Printed in China through Worldprint Ltd.

12 13 14 15 16   10 9 8 7 6 5 4 3 2 1

COVER IMAGE
An Observer aboard a German bomber gets a close-up
view of a British Spitfire fighter plane during the Battle of
Britain, 1940.

TITLE PAGE IMAGE
The iconic image of a fighter pilot published on the cover
of *Picture Post* at the height of the Battle of Britain, August
1940.

CONTENTS PAGE IMAGE
RAF wings brooch presented by a Battle of Britain pilot to
his sweetheart.

DEDICATION
For Alex

ACKNOWLEDGEMENTS
I am grateful for all the help and support of many people
in the production of this little volume. In particular I
would like to record my thanks to: Peter Murton, Sue
Chippington and Philip Sawford at Imperial War Museum
Duxford; Andrew Cormack at RAF Museum Hendon;
Fleet Air Arm Museum, RNAS Yeovilton, Somerset; Mick
Jennings, Bob Collis, Robin Housego, Colin and Rachel
Stonebridge, Squadron Leader J. R. Love, and the late Air
Marshal Sir Denis Crowley-Milling who was the first to
encourage my research into the Battle of Britain.

Illustrations in this volume are from the author's
collection, or are from other sources as follows:

The Imperial War Museum, pages 7 (both), 8, 11
(bottom), 12, 19 (bottom), 21 (bottom), 22, 23, 26, 27,
29, 30, 31, 32 (both), 33, 34, 37, 38, 39 (bottom), 42, 43
(bottom), 44, 45, 47 (top), 50, 54 (bottom) and 53
(both); Mary Evans Picture Collection, cover and pages 16
(bottom) and 18 (bottom); Osprey Publishing, page 24;
RAF Museum Hendon, page 52.

IMPERIAL WAR MUSEUM COLLECTIONS
Some of the photos in this book come from the Imperial
War Museum's huge collections which cover all aspects of
conflict involving Britain and the Commonwealth since the
start of the twentieth century. These rich resources are
available online to search, browse and buy at
www.iwmcollections.org.uk. In addition to Collections
Online, you can visit the Visitor Rooms where you can
explore over 8 million photographs, thousands of hours of
moving images, the largest sound archive of its kind in the
world, thousands of diaries and letters written by people
in wartime, and a huge reference library. To make an
appointment, call (020) 7416 5320, or e-mail
mail@iwm.org.uk. Imperial War Museum
www.iwm.org.uk

Shire Publications is supporting the Woodland Trust, the UK's leading woodland conservation charity, by funding the dedication of trees.

CONTENTS

FLIGHT, JANUARY 19, 1939

REGD AT THE G.P.O. AS A NEWSPA

FIRST AERO WEEKLY IN THE WORLD

FLIGHT

6

No. 1569
Vol. XXXV

The
AIRCRAFT ENGINEER

OFFICIAL ORGAN OF THE ROYAL AERO CLUB

ROLLS-ROYCE AERO ENGINES FOR SPEED AND RELIABILITY

PRELUDE

WHEN ADOLF HITLER became Chancellor of Germany in 1933 he withdrew Germany from the League of Nations and announced his plans to expand the German military forces far beyond the limitations stipulated in the Treaty of Versailles. Although Britain and other countries protested, no country took direct action to stop him; many knew that aircraft technology had advanced far beyond the fighter and bomber biplanes of the First World War and feared what might happen in the future. In that same year H. G. Wells published *The Shape of Things to Come* in which, albeit fictionally, he explored the potential changes in the nature of warfare, notably aerial warfare, and included harrowing descriptions of cities destroyed by bombing. Wells articulated a groundswell of public concern about air attacks; in October 1933 plans for the enlargement of the British Air Defence Intelligence System were announced and the Observer Corps expanded.

In September 1935 Prime Minister Stanley Baldwin issued a circular entitled 'Air Raid Precautions' (ARP), which invited local authorities to set up working committees and undertake measures such as the construction of public shelters to protect the populace, but little action was undertaken at that time; events in 1936 were to change matters, when Hitler reoccupied the demilitarised zone in the Rhineland and sent military forces to assist General Franco during the Spanish Civil War. The Luftwaffe's bombing of Madrid in November 1936 and the bombing of Guernica in April 1937 caused international horror and revulsion, and left no one in any doubt that if another war were to come – and as each year passed it seemed increasingly inevitable – air power would play a significant role in it.

Like many decisions made by those in positions of power before the outbreak of the Second World War, the expansion of Britain's military forces was left until the eleventh hour, despite pleas being made from all three services from the mid-1930s. The Royal Air Force, the service that was to become the key to Britain's victory in the Battle of Britain, was no exception. The decision to undertake an expansion of the RAF was made in 1935 and work had begun on the re-activation and development of some of the First

Opposite:
Cover of *Flight*
magazine from
January 1939
advertising
Rolls-Royce Aero
Engines; the power
house for both the
Hawker Hurricane
and the
Supermarine
Spitfire.

5

World War airfields but the major recruitment drive for RAF and RAFVR personnel to fly, crew and maintain the planes did not occur until 1939. Only in July 1939 was it announced that new RAFVR recruitment and training centres were to open across the country, and appeals appeared in the press for volunteers pilots, air observers and wireless operator air gunners.

The creation of a Royal Air Force Volunteer Reserve of pilots had been announced in July 1936. In many ways a 'Territorial Army of the Air', membership was extended to those with no experience of flying. They would train during certain evenings in the week and at weekends at a network of aerodromes established near large population centres. Ground instruction would be provided at locations in large towns or cities while the aerodromes, run by civilian contractors who usually employed members of the Reserve of Air Force Officers (RAFO) as instructors, provided the practical training flights for the potential pilots. (Members of the RAFO had previously completed a four-year Short Service Commission as pilots in the RAF.) Candidates received a retaining fee of £25 per year and appropriate allowances while under training.

Lapel badge for members of the Royal Air Force Volunteer Reserve while in civilian clothes.

There were also University Air Squadrons, at Oxford, Cambridge and London, for example, in which former pupils of public schools such as Eton College were well represented. In addition, Short Service Commissions were available to candidates who had some flying experience, allowing them to hone their skills within the sphere of military flying and combat training; a number of the pilots who joined this scheme came from colonies such as Canada and Australia. Others applied for enrolment into the Empire Training Scheme and undertook their training in Canada. Many of the pilots from across the colonies and those who had escaped from Nazi-occupied countries such as Poland or Czechoslovakia were to serve as pilots with the RAF during the Battle of Britain. In war time the Volunteer Reserve would become the principal means of entry into the RAF, with all commissions in the General Duties (Flying) Branch being given to men from the ranks of the RAFVR.

The distinctive 'VR' badge worn on the lapels of the uniforms of RAFVR Officers.

War broke out on 3 September 1939; the first units of the British Expeditionary Force landed in France in the early hours of 21 September and took up positions near the Belgian border. Although Britain was at war with Germany it all seemed very distant to civilians at home. During the months between September and early May 1940 few contacts occurred between the Allied and German forces, and the squadrons of German aircraft droning

Sergeant Geoffrey 'Sammy' Allard of No. 85 Squadron RAF being congratulated on his return to Lille-Seclin in France on the evening of 10 May 1940, after shooting down the second of two Heinkel He 111s claimed by him that day. (IWM C 1512)

over Britain – blasting London to rubble in less than a week, as some predicted – did not emerge. A few mines were dropped along the coastline by German long-range bombers but there were no bombs on the mainland and no casualties; indeed more accidents and fatalities were caused by the blackouts than by enemy action. Many children who had been evacuated returned home for Christmas, and dissenting voices in Britain began to question the necessity of being on a war footing in this country at all. The general attitude of many British citizens during this time was best summed up by the American press who dubbed it 'the phoney war.'

Air Chief Marshal Hugh Dowding, Air Officer Commander-in-Chief Fighter Command during the Battle of Britain. (IWM D 1417)

This illusion was shattered on 10 May 1940 when Hitler unleashed his *Blitzkrieg* (literally meaning 'lightning war'). Belgium and Luxembourg were invaded and fell rapidly; on 12 May Panzer divisions rolled into Holland and the BEF fell back along the River Dyle. When the German offensive began the RAF had a total of 2,750 front-line aircraft, about a thousand of which were fighters. Over the period of 11–12 May four additional RAF fighter squadrons had been sent to France, followed by a further thirty-two Hurricanes which flew over on 13 May; thus about a third of the entire RAF fighter force committed to

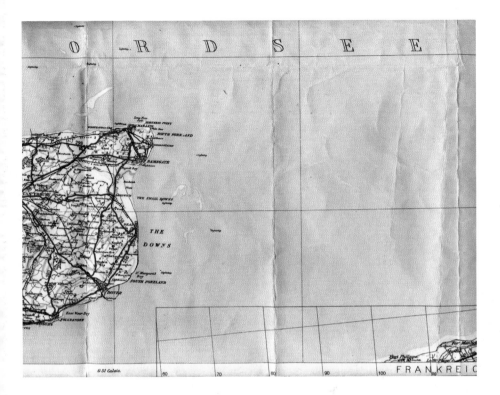

operations in France. As early as 14 May 1940 General Brooke had ordered a retreat from the River Dendre to the River Schultz while Air Chief Marshal Hugh Dowding, Air Officer Commander-in-Chief Fighter Command, raised his concerns about losses of British fighter aircraft in France, pointing out at a Cabinet meeting that if the rate of attrition continued for another two weeks there would not be a single Hurricane left in France or Britain.

The situation in France rapidly deteriorated and fears over the defences of Britain were raised. On 16 May 1940 Dowding wrote to the Under Secretary of State for Air, Harold Balfour, explaining his concerns over the depletion of aircraft and requesting that he consider 'as a matter of paramount urgency what level of strength is to be left for the defences of this country, and ... assure me that when this level has been reached, not one fighter will be sent across the channel'. Dowding had to fight against political opposition but his plea was heard and Churchill gave the controversial order that no more fighters should leave British shores. The men of the BEF would curse the lack of air cover but the decision preserved the core of home fighter defence that was to be so desperately needed to fight the Battle of Britain.

German invasion map showing the Dover area and the tip of the French coast, 1940.

Opposite: Troops evacuated from Dunkirk wait to leave their ship at Dover, 31 May 1940. (IWM H 1628)

9

A German
propaganda
publication on
the bombing of
Great Britain.

Churchill told the War Cabinet on 20 May that he had recommended the Chiefs of Staff to prepare a study for the covering operations in the event of it being necessary to withdraw the British Expeditionary Force from France. Deep in the galleries below Dover Castle, Vice-Admiral Bertram Ramsey, Flag Officer Dover, inaugurated a discussion on the emergency evacuation across the channel of a very large force. Over the next few days the Admiralty began to amass shipping for a possible evacuation of the BEF and Allied forces from France. Originally planned as an evacuation from three ports, after the fall of Boulogne and Calais only Dunkirk was left. On 25 May the War Cabinet sanctioned the BEF's march north to Dunkirk. On 26 May 1940 the War Cabinet despatched a signal sent via the Admiralty to Ramsey reading simply: 'Operation *Dynamo* is to commence.'

Between 26 May and 4 June 1940 the beleaguered British Expeditionary Force was evacuated from the beaches of Dunkirk in Operation *Dynamo*. Despite the references to a 'fighting retreat' and the story of the noble 'little ships', Dunkirk was not just an evacuation – it also heralded a defeat for the BEF. On 18 June Churchill grimly announced in Parliament: 'What General Weygand called the Battle of France is over. I expect that the Battle of Britain is about to begin.'

By the time France capitulated on 25 June many British households had already received the leaflet entitled *If the Invader Comes*. The people of Britain were left under no illusions and stood with their backs to the wall; despite obtaining support from loyal colonies and receiving supplies from America, many felt that Britain faced the enemy alone with only 22 miles of Channel separating them from the 'Nazi hordes'.

Luftwaffe technical dictionary from 1940 in German/English/French.

British army sentries keep a lonely vigil over the Channel from the White Cliffs, 1940. (IWM H 5108)

MEN AND MACHINES

THE TRAINING PROCESS

The story of any pilot begins with his recruitment and training. In Britain during the Second World War, the RAFVR became the principal means of entry into the RAF; all commissions in the General Duties (Flying) Branch were given to men from its ranks. Those called up who volunteered for the RAF and were found fit, with their eyesight good enough to train as pilots, would become cadets. Cadets were sent to the reception units of the Initial Training Wing (ITW) where they would undergo drill training, learn Morse code and administration, and attend lectures on such topics as air navigation, gunnery and mathematics. If the cadet demonstrated competence and *esprit de corps* he would pass out from ITW and would be sent to an Elementary Flying Training School (EFTS). Here he would be given flying kit and a parachute and begin to train in the art of flying, often in De Havilland Tiger Moths or Miles Magisters, affectionately known as 'Maggies'. Recording his flying hours in his log book, after about two or three weeks a young pilot should show progress and confidence in his flying skills and would then be transferred to a Service Flying Training Squadron, where fledgling pilots were taught advanced aerobatics, as well as carrying out longer flights and practice landings. He would complete his training with an Operational Training Unit, and would proudly leave this final training establishment to join his Operational Squadron, wearing his RAF trained pilot wings on his jacket. The RAF's aim was to train men to fly over a minimum period of eight to ten weeks, but of course, in time of war and need, the time and extent of training could be a lot less.

Opposite: Battle of Britain ace, Group Captain A. G. 'Sailor' Malan, No. 74 Squadron RAF. (IWM CH 008119)

Below: *Taking Off* – an inspirational booklet for aspiring pilots.

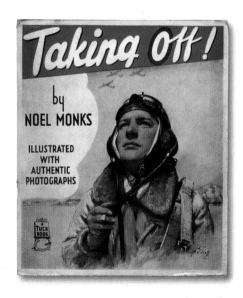

The Luftwaffe also had a stringent regime for the recruitment of suitable candidates to be pilots: they would be sent to air academies where an average German pilot student received almost 250 flight hours of training, including about eighty hours in operational aircraft. The Luftwaffe's participation in the Spanish Civil War also meant that its active combat and bombing experience was far more up to date than that of its British counterparts; however, the Luftwaffe's fatal flaw was that its instructor pilots were looked upon first and foremost as front-line pilots who undertook some training, rather than as full-time instructors. Retaining only a comparatively small reserve of pilots, as losses mounted more instructors were posted to operational units and training suffered as a result.

Operational RAF fighter squadrons were commanded by an officer holding the rank of Squadron Leader; each squadron consisted of two flights – A and B – each of which was commanded by a Flight Lieutenant. Each flight was divided into Red, Green and Yellow sections, with three aircraft in each. During the Battle a total of sixty-eight squadrons of Fighter Command operated from thirty-five airfields across the country. Thirty-five of the squadrons were equipped with Hurricanes, nineteen with Spitfires, and the remainder predominantly with Blenheims.

THE AIRCRAFT

The two main fighter aircraft used by the RAF during the Battle of Britain were the Hawker Hurricane and the Supermarine Spitfire. The Hurricane Mk I had done sterling service as early as

Top: The eagle worn on the tunics of all Luftwaffe officers.

Middle: The collar rank insignia of a Luftwaffe lieutenant. The yellow facing denoted flying personnel.

Bottom: Luftwaffe pilot qualification breast badge.

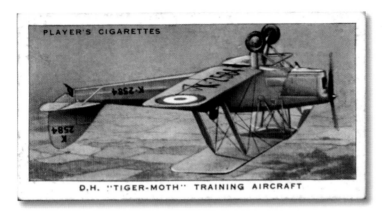

The de Havilland 'Tiger Moth' training aircraft.

PLAYER'S CIGARETTES

D.H. "TIGER-MOTH" TRAINING AIRCRAFT

October 1939 and during the Battle of France. It had a Rolls-Royce Merlin II engine with a top speed of 335 mph at 17,500 feet and was armed with four .303 Browning machine guns in each wing. The Hurricane was remembered by those who flew it as a 'damn good gun platform' with a tight turning radius

HAVE YOU RECEIVED
1 GREATCOAT
1 JACKET
2 PAIRS TROUSERS
1 CAP
2 SHIRTS
4 COLLARS
2 PAIRS BOOTS
1 PAIR SHOES, CANVAS WITH LACES
3 PAIRS LACES
SIGN OUTSIDE
NO DEFICIENCIES ADMITTED AFTER LEAVING

A new-intake cadet pilot collects his kit from stores.

The Miles 'Magister' training aircraft.

PLAYER'S CIGARETTES

MILES "MAGISTER" TRAINING AIRCRAFT

and a fine reputation for ruggedness, having brought a number of pilots back to their base despite being badly damaged. The main drawbacks of the Hurricane were its thick wings, which compromised acceleration, and the wood and fabric coverings of its rear fuselage, making the aircraft prone to fire. The gravity fuel tank in the forward fuselage, immediately behind the instrument panel, was particularly notorious for sending a jet of flame through the panel onto the pilot if the aircraft was on fire or if the tank was ignited by

Good advice for young pilots!

Keep a good look-out!

PILOTS: Look-on both sides where you are going
M.T. DRIVERS: Keep well clear of Taxi Tracks and give way to Aircraft

FOLLOW ME
STOP

RAF 36

a hit from a bullet. As a consequence a number of Hurricane pilots were badly burned (many of them became early members of the 'Guinea Pig Club', formed in 1941 by those who had undergone reconstructive plastic surgery). In spite of performance deficiencies, especially against the Messerschmitt Bf 109, the Hurricane was still capable of destroying the German fighter and others, especially at lower altitudes. The thirty-five RAF squadrons that fought with Hurricanes could proudly say it was the Hawker Hurricane that brought down more enemy planes during the Battle of Britain than any other.

The Supermarine Spitfire entered RAF service with No. 19 Squadron at Duxford in 1938. Instantly recognisable for the combination of its sleek design, elliptical wings and distinctive sound of the Rolls Royce Merlin II engine that powered many of them, it could climb well and with a maximum speed of 367 mph it was the fastest single-seater fighter in service. The majority of Spitfires in 1940 were armed with four .303 Browning machine guns but to increase the 'killing power' of its guns, thirty Spitfires armed with a Hispano cannon in each wing were delivered to No. 19 Squadron in June 1940. (Due to problems, especially stoppages, it was only in August 1940 that the modified, and far more efficient,

Spitfire brooch fashioned from an old penny.

Part-section diagram of the Hawker Hurricane.

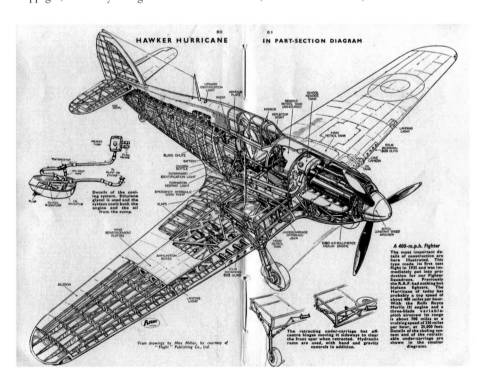

HAWKER HURRICANE IN PART-SECTION DIAGRAM

From drawings by Max Millar, by courtesy of "Flight" Publishing Co., Ltd.

A 400-m.p.h. Fighter

The most important details of construction are here illustrated. This type made its first test flight in 1935 and was immediately put into production for our Fighter Squadrons. Previously the R.A.F. had nothing but biplane fighters. The Hurricane of today has probably a top speed of about 400 miles per hour. With the Rolls Royce Merlin III engine and a three-blade variable-pitch airscrew its range is about 700 miles at a cruising speed of 230 miles per hour, at 25,000 feet. Details of the cooling system and of the retractable under-carriage are shown in the smaller diagrams.

The retracting under-carriage has off-centre hinges moving it sideways to clear the front spar when retracted. Hydraulic rams are used, with hand and gravity controls in addition.

Above left: RAF officer's cap badge.

Above right: The much-prized wings of a Royal Air Force pilot.

Below: Part-section diagram of a Messerschmitt Bf 109 (also known as the ME 109).

Spitfires with Hispanos entered regular service.) The beautiful Spitfire inspired confidence in its pilots and was loved by them, many believing it was this aircraft that really took the fight back against the enemy; despite being supplied to only nineteen RAF squadrons during the Battle of Britain, it had a lower attrition rate and a higher victory-to-loss ratio than the Hurricanes. Its place in history was further assured by the eulogistic promotion it received across all media during the famous Spitfire Fund organised by Lord Beaverbrook. The Spitfire was the only British fighter to remain in production throughout the war.

The predominant Luftwaffe aircraft in the Battle of Britain were the Dornier 17, Heinkel He 111 and Junkers Ju 88 bombers; the Junkers

Ju 87 'Stuka' dive bombers; and the Messerschmitt Bf 109 and Bf 110 fighters. Both the fighters and bombers were equipped with 7.9 mm machine guns, comparable with the machine guns of the RAF; the Messerschmitt, however, carried heavy-hitting 20 mm cannons but was hampered by its short range and as a consequence, like all the other Luftwaffe aircraft in the Battle, would only have a short time in the combat zone. Messerschmitt pilots were ever mindful of rapidly decreasing fuel levels, something the RAF fighter pilots frequently used to their advantage.

A DAY IN THE LIFE OF AN RAF FIGHTER PILOT

An RAF fighter pilot's daily routine could literally mean 'daily', because at times during the height of the Battle it was not always possible for pilots to have a regular day off. An officer pilot would begin his day at dawn when his batman brought him a cup of tea; Sergeant Pilots would wake themselves up and make their own. After time to wash, shave and dress, the lorry would arrive to collect all aircrew and drive them out to the dispersals, a short distance from their fighter aircraft, beside the grass runways. Most of these areas would have 'readiness huts' or at least a couple of bell tents where some breakfast would be prepared. Meanwhile the Flight Commander would ring through to Operations to report his men ready.

Above: RAF Other Ranks and Junior NCOs cap badge.

Below: Pilots and gunners of No. 264 Squadron RAF pass the time with a game of draughts while waiting at readiness outside their dispersal tent at Kirton-in-Lindsey, Lincolnshire. (IWM CH 868)

A 1932-pattern 'Mae West' life vest, as worn during the Battle of Britain. With so many men ditching in the channel these life vests were sometimes painted yellow to make the ditched pilot more visible. This innovation was soon adopted in manufacture and later in the war vests were produced in a yellow material.

Fleece-lined 1936-pattern flying boots.

Leather gauntlets worn by fighter pilots.

Leather B-Type flying helmet and Mk IVb goggles.

The pilots themselves often dressed in a motley selection of flying suits and four-pocket tunics with a mix of cravats at the collar (flying in a collar and tie is not comfortable), flying boots and life vests. Some would be wearing their side cap, peaked cap, or perhaps, if just seated around the dispersal area, no hat at all. Their seating might comprise canvas or Lloyd Loom chairs; some lucky chaps might even have had sofas and armchairs. There were card tables suitable for a game of dominoes, chequers or chess, or for parking mugs of tea. There might even be a gramophone for some music. They might read books or magazines and there were plenty of cigarettes and pipes too. But beneath this relaxed façade they would be tensely awaiting the tannoy or bell that would announce a 'scramble'. The bells were often unofficially painted with messages such as, 'If you hear the bell – run like hell!'

RAF Edition (War) map. Pilots often tucked these into their boots for easy access.

Upon hearing the Scramble, the pilots and ground crews would all know their duties and run to get the fighters in the air as quickly as possible, the pilots knocking their hats off on the way so they could get in the cockpit, pull on helmet and goggles (left on the gun sight) and strap in to the cockpit. The headphones in the helmet would relay information from the senior pilot pertinent to the bearing of the enemy – their altitude and numbers – as the fitter pressed the starter button on the nearby battery carts to start the engine. The pilot would then give a thumbs up, signalling that all was well and that all ground crew should ensure they were clear of the aircraft. The pilot would then push the throttle, taxi his fighter to the grass runway and take off.

Once in the air more specific directions would be issued and the pilots would be looking for sight of the enemy such as condensation trails or the

Scramble given, the pilots run to their aircraft at an RAF fighter base, July 1940. (IWM HU 49253)

aircraft themselves. Their aim was to draw away and pick off the German fighters and attack the bombers before they reached their targets.

Whilst there were overall directives concerning strategies in dogfights, these evolved and changed rapidly in response to experience. Throughout the course of the Battle of Britain tactics varied at all levels, from group to group and squadron to squadron, right down to individual pilots. One tactic that became widely used was the 'finger four' formation consisting of a lead element and a second element, each element comprising two aircraft. The two elements were spaced in an order similar to the fingertips on a right hand (hence the name). The flight leader in the lead element would head the formation with one wingman to his rear left. The second element would be made up of the other two planes, the element leader and his wingman. Both the flight leader and element leader would have offensive roles and would be the ones to open fire on enemy aircraft while the flight remained intact; each of their wingmen would act in a defensive role, covering the rear of each of the leaders.

The effectiveness of a pilot's attack depended on speed: it was calculated that a pilot had only three seconds or so in which to identify and engage his enemy before the opportunity was lost. Maintaining a clear head and spotting the enemy fighters was essential – no mean feat at 30,000 feet in an unpressurised cockpit, with basic flying clothing, no heating and a mass of noise in your ears from radio traffic, your own engine, the engines of all the aircraft around you and from the hammering of your eight Browning machine guns in the wings, firing at the rate of 13 pounds of shot every three seconds. During a fight the G-forces caused by manoeuvring, whether to engage or escape from an enemy aircraft, could lead to the brain becoming starved of blood, provoking the nightmare scenario of suffering a blackout.

As noted above, the method of attack varied from squadron to squadron: some specialised in effective but extremely dangerous head-on attacks against the German bombers; in others, the fighters would dive through the enemy bomber formation. Attacking from the side was also popular against bombers and, with good timing and skill, the side of the bomber could be raked with gun fire. The favoured attack method was with the sun behind; with the sun in his eyes, the enemy could be taken unawares and could find it tricky to take aim. Luftwaffe pilots also used this method – hence the warning drummed into all fighter pilots, 'Beware the Hun in the sun!'

If a pilot were to be hit and his aircraft incapacitated he had just seconds to decide if he could attempt a landing in a nearby field or if he would need to bail out. Again, the G-force as the plane plummeted down (sometimes in a dreaded spin) would be enormous; to bail out and deploy his parachute, the pilot would need to open the canopy of his aircraft against the G-force keeping him in his seat. Of course, not all pilots parachuted onto land. Those who ended up 'in the drink' would have to work fast to get rid of their parachutes when they hit the water, lest they be dragged down by them.

On average, engagement with the enemy would last about ten minutes, but in the speed and intensity of aerial combat, a second could seem like hours. If a pilot was lucky enough to survive the action and return, his duty would be to file a combat report with full details of the sortie, recording any 'kills' (enemy aircraft shot down). This could be just one of two or three such sorties flown in a single day during the Battle of Britain. A pilot would undoubtedly look around him each time he returned from a sortie: perhaps he had seen his pal shot down; perhaps he would only learn of the loss from another member of the flight, a gap where his plane should have been, or an empty space at the dinner table. Once the sun set, the flight would be stood down. Sometimes pilots might muster the energy for a trip to the pub, but many would simply hit the sack soon after dinner, exhausted, to sleep as best they could until the next dawn call.

Opposite: Sequence of camera gun still frames showing the destruction of a Bf 110 by a British fighter during the Battle of Britain. (IWM C 2433)

Left: Flight Sergeant G. C. 'Grumpy' Unwin of No. 19 Squadron RAF climbs out of his Supermarine Spitfire Mark I at Fowlmere, Cambridgeshire, after a sortie. Unwin shot down more than fourteen enemy aircraft between May and September 1940. (IWM CH 1355)

THE BATTLE

THE BATTLE OF BRITAIN, when viewed from a British perspective, is officially recognised as having taken place from 10 July to 31 October 1940. Historians have described the Battle in a variety of ways but in general it is viewed in five phases. Precise dates vary because each phase often blended into the next. From the German standpoint, the opening of the Battle of Britain commenced on what they called *Adler Tag* (Eagle Day) on 13 August 1940, when the Luftwaffe began its attacks on the RAF Fighter Command airfields and air defence network. During the course of this day the Luftwaffe conducted 1,500 sorties, shot down thirteen RAF fighters and destroyed a further forty-seven upon six airfields. Britain's defences did not fail her and shot down forty-six enemy aircraft. For Germany, the Battle of Britain continued throughout the Blitz until they changed tack and launched a massive attack upon Soviet Russia in June 1941.

PHASE 1: 26 JUNE TO 16 JULY, 1940

Having conquered France the Luftwaffe used the latter part of June 1940 to settle into its occupied airfields in Norway, Belgium, France and the Netherlands, rested and refitted many of its squadrons and regrouped its fighter Fliegerkorps in readiness for the forthcoming attacks on Britain. By July 1940 Luftflotte 2 and 3 had 2,075 aircraft consisting of nine hundred fighters, 875 bombers and three hundred dive bombers while Luftflotte 5 in Norway and Denmark stood poised to attack along the eastern seaboard of Britain, equipped with 123 bombers and 300 dive bombers. Having had but a few weeks to lick its wounds after Dunkirk the RAF had just forty-six fighter squadrons (two of which were equipped with the unsatisfactory Boulton Paul Defiant, which was soon to be transferred to the night fighter role) with four more squadrons in the course of formation. The RAF could muster between six hundred and seven hundred aircraft with 1,253 pilots.

Although the BEF returned in a beleaguered state from France in May 1940, it is often forgotten that the Royal Navy remained largely intact and any invasion fleet would have it to contend with. Supplies shipped in by

Opposite:
A vivid depiction of Acting Flight Lieutenant Peter Brothers' aerial combat with two Bf 109Es while flying his No. 32 Squadron Hurricane over the English Channel, off Dover on 20 July 1940.

25

Merchant Navy convoys, although menaced by U-boats, did get through so it was offensive patrols by the Luftwaffe against shipping in the English Channel and coastal targets along the South and East coasts that marked the opening phase of the Battle of Britain in July 1940. The Luftwaffe attacks on 4 July sank four freighters and damage was inflicted on others, so as a direct result the Channel was closed to large merchant ships setting off to cross the Atlantic.

The day officially recognised as the commencement of the Battle of Britain was Wednesday 10 July 1940. The first encounter occurred after the Spitfires of 66 Squadron, based at the newly opened RAF Coltishall in Norfolk, took off at 04:40 hrs. Climbing to 15,000 feet Sergeant F. N. Robertson, flying Spitfire N3035 and accompanied by two other Spitfires, intercepted a lone Dornier 17z from Kampfgeschwader 3 in the skies over Winterton, Norfolk. The gunner of the enemy aircraft successfully hit one of the Spitfires, forcing him to return to base, but the remaining pair continued the assault until Sergeant Robertson brought home his attack against the Dornier and it crashed into the sea. Luftflotten 2, 3 and 5 persisted with a number of small-scale night and day raids that tested British defences and allowed the Germans to gather final intelligence before their proposed invasion of Britain.

During this opening phase of the Battle a number of inexperienced young RAF pilots were lost when they got their blood up and pursued their Luftwaffe quarries back towards France only to be 'jumped' by Bf109s over

Heinkel He 111s in formation – a poor match against Hurricanes and Spitfires during the Battle. (IWM MH 6547)

the sea. The aerial combat over the coastal convoys was vicious and costly to both sides; the enemy raiders often greatly outnumbered the comparatively small number of fighters the RAF could send up against them but RAF fighters consistently brought down and damaged more German aircraft than they lost.

PHASE 2: 17 JULY TO 12 AUGUST

In War Directive No. 16 of 16 July 1940 Adolf Hitler stated: 'The English Air Force must be so reduced morally and physically that it is unable to deliver any significant attack against the German crossing [of the English Channel].' The Luftwaffe was ordered to be in a state of readiness from 17 July and focused on its two main tasks to pave the way for the invasion: firstly to gain a stranglehold over Britain by intensifying its attacks on shipping and ports; secondly to eliminate the RAF in the air and on the ground, including the destruction of the Home Defence system and the aircraft industry. On 19 July Hitler made his infamous 'Last Appeal to Reason' speech before the Reichstag – it was even translated into English and printed on leaflets that were dropped over England by the Luftwaffe. Despite earlier dissenting voices in Government that argued for appeasement, Winston Churchill had stood firm and summed up the British resolve in his speech to the House of Commons on 4 June 1940:

Aircrew of No. 22 Squadron RAF walking away from their Bristol Beaufort Mark Is after a mission, at North Coates, Lincolnshire, 19 July 1940. (IWM CH 639)

A LAST APPEAL TO REASON

BY

ADOLF HITLER

Speech before the Reichstag, 19th July, 1940

World War Enemies Unscrupulous Victors

Britain and France Considered Understanding a Crime

German propaganda leaflet dropped over Britain featuring an English translation of Hitler's speech to the German Reichstag of 19 July 1940.

> We shall fight on the seas and oceans, we shall fight with growing confidence and growing strength in the air, we shall defend our island, whatever the cost may be. We shall fight on the beaches, we shall fight on the landing grounds, we shall fight in the fields and in the streets, we shall fight in the hills; we shall never surrender.

The four weeks of this phase, known as the *Kanalkampf* (the Channel battles) to the Germans, saw the aircraft of Luftflotten 2 and 3 conduct more frequent and larger bombing and mine-laying missions on the convoys and shipping lanes across the English Channel, along with ports and coastal airfields and along the south-east coast and the Straits of Dover. This latter location along the south-eastern tip of England was the front line, and fell prey to the strafing runs of low-flying Bf 109s. RAF bases in this area such as Manston and Rochford (Southend) were soon liberally pitted with bomb craters, as were many other military installations and locations that drew enemy attacks, to the extent that it was soon dubbed 'Hellfire Corner'.

During this same period other missions saw Luftwaffe aircraft probe further inland to goad the RAF fighters into action and attack RAF airfields, installations and factories in the Midlands and along the east coast. It was also during this phase that the first large-scale attack was launched against radar stations and the first target upon the British mainland, the Portland Naval Base, on 11 August 1940. Three RAF squadrons were scrambled to attack the raiders while another seven were put in the air to patrol Weymouth. About 150 enemy aircraft were engaged in the attack and massive dogfights took place as the enemy raiders pressed home their attack upon the docks, oil tanks, gas works and barracks. At the end of this single engagement the Luftwaffe had lost thirty-eight aircraft; the RAF thirty-two.

The following day the Luftwaffe raiders returned again, attacking Portsmouth, radar stations and coastal airfields. RAF Hawkinge and Manston were badly hit. German Intelligence claimed that seventy Spitfires and Hurricanes had been destroyed, including the complete destruction of

Fighter pilots of No. 610 Squadron, Royal Air Force relaxing between sorties at Hawkinge July 1940. (IWM HU 001062)

65 Squadron at Manston. The Spitfires of this squadron had indeed been bombed by the Dorniers of Kampfgeschwader 2 while they were taxiing out for take-off but in reality had, in the main, managed to get airborne amid the bomb bursts.

Armed not only with erroneous information about the losses of British fighters but also with inaccurate and misleading interpretation of information gathered from reconnaissance missions, German High Command confidence was high on the eve of Eagle Day.

PHASE 3: 13 AUGUST TO 6 SEPTEMBER

As noted previously, from a German standpoint the Battle of Britain commenced on 13 August 1940 when the Luftwaffe began their concerted attack. The initial aim was to force Fighter Command out of the south-eastern corner of England within four days and to effect complete destruction of the RAF within four weeks, thus removing any airborne opposition to the planned invasion.

On this first day Luftflotten 2 and 3 flew 485 bomber and one thousand fighter sorties, the highest number to date. The sheer number of enemy aircraft in the air was staggering to the RAF pilots but they carried on undaunted: on this day forty-five German aircraft were brought down for just thirteen RAF fighters and out of these, although some were wounded, ten RAF pilots were saved. On 15 August Luftflotte 5 began raids against targets in the north-east of Britain from its base in Norway, and over the following weeks the Luftwaffe conducted a constant stream of attacks on airfields and installations during daylight hours, while maintaining attacks against shipping, ports and aircraft factories at night.

Flight Lieutenant Eric James Brindley Nicolson, the only RAF VC awarded during the Battle of Britain for aerial combat action near Southampton on 16 August 1940. (IWM CH 1700)

In the aerial combats, which regularly saw twelve RAF fighters against a hundred or more Luftwaffe aircraft, the pilots of the RAF fought on undaunted. It was during this phase that the hardest-fought day of the Battle of Britain took place, on Sunday 18 August when the Luftwaffe made its most concentrated attack, aiming to destroy or permanently cripple RAF Fighter Command airfields. It was a clear and beautiful English summer morning when the first sixty Heinkel He 111s attacked Biggin Hill and a mixed group of forty-eight Junkers Ju 88s and Dornier Do 17s attacked Kenley, which alone received a hundred bombs. Further attacks followed upon Croydon, Hawkinge and West Malling.

During the afternoon a further three large raids were attempted, the first and third by mixed groups of bombers escorted by a mixture of enemy fighters, predominantly Messerschmitt Bf 109s, Bf 110s and Stuka

Air Vice Marshal Keith Park, Commander of No. 11 Group RAF. (IWM CM 003513)

dive bombers, which targeted the RAF airfields at Thorney Island and Gosport, as well as the Fleet Air Arm fighter station at Ford in Sussex and the radar station at Poling. In the late afternoon the raiders returned to attack Croydon again and twelve 109s tore in below the radar to attack RAF Manston, destroying two Spitfires on the ground, killing an airman and injuring fifteen others. The airfields, however, had been doggedly defended and during the course of the day the RAF had lost thirty-four aircraft in the air and twenty-nine on the ground whilst the Luftwaffe lost sixty-nine.

Although the airfields of southern England received regular assaults and suffered a lot of damage, RAF Fighter Command continued to cause serious and unexpected losses to the Luftwaffe at a time when it had been anticipated by German intelligence that the men and resources of the RAF would be exhausted. However, it was a close-run thing and Fighter Command's reserves were running dangerously low: between 26 August and 6 September, RAF losses stood at 248, the Luftwaffe's 322. Air Vice Marshal Keith Park, the commander of No. 11 Group RAF responsible for the fighter defence of London and south-east England, was only too aware of the dangerous situation caused by exuberant young pilots engaging enemy fighters that posed no major threat to Britain. He made it clear that his fighters had to target the bombers to stop them bombing his airfields.

PHASE 4: 7 SEPTEMBER TO
2 OCTOBER

Tower Bridge
and the Tower
of London on the
first day of the
Blitz on the capital.
(IWM HU 653)

On 3 September 1940, the first anniversary of the outbreak of the war, Hermann Göring confidently addressed his commanders:

> We are now on the brink of victory. Our intelligence has ... informed us that the RAF is now down to less than a hundred fighter aircraft, the airfields protecting London are out of action because of the superb and accurate bombing of our bomber force ....The next target must be London itself.

Reichsmarschall
Hermann Göring.
(IWM MH 6041)

During September there was a distinct change of tactics in the air. Göring believed the last reserve of Fighter Command could be drawn into battle and destroyed if the Luftwaffe turned upon London as a primary target. German High Command was also keen to support this because they believed that by bringing London to its knees, morale would be crippled and the British would be more likely to discuss terms. (It should not be forgotten that other population centres and places of industry across Britain were also attacked or suffered as a result of enemy action during this time.)

London had suffered an air raid on 6 September 1940 but the first major day of the air offensive on London with Reichsmarschall Hermann Göring in direct command was 7 September 1940, a beautifully

A Heinkel He 111 bomber flying over Wapping and the Isle of Dogs in the East End of London at the start of the Luftwaffe's evening raids of 7 September 1940. (IWM C 5422)

clear summer's day. Luftwaffe aircraft had been spotted on reconnaissance flights over a number of places across Britain including Liverpool, Manchester, Yorkshire and East Anglia but during the afternoon about 350 enemy bombers escorted by hundreds of fighters were spotted making for the Thames Estuary. At 16:35 the first bombs fell on the Ford motor works at Dagenham, followed by a massive drop of both high explosive and incendiary bombs upon Beckton Gas Works, at the time the largest in Europe; this was followed by the bombing of the London Docks, factories, warehouses and rows of terraced houses and tenements in the East End. Soon the flames and huge columns of greasy black and grey smoke were billowing skyward from Woolwich to Tower Bridge. By 18:00 the enemy raiders had gone but despite the best efforts of the fire crews (six hundred were ordered to West Ham alone) the fires blazed into the night and guided wave after wave of Heinkel and Dornier bombers to their target until dawn the following day, when the enemy raiders finally droned off leaving large areas of the East End ablaze and smashed to rubble. When the final toll of the day that became known as Black Saturday was counted, 436 men, women and children had been killed and around 1,600 badly injured. So ended the first day of the Blitz, a sustained bombing campaign against

London and other British cities with towns, villages and homesteads all around facing the danger of stray bombs.

For the following fifty-seven days London was bombed in raids conducted both during the day and at night. Life during that time could be fraught, dangerous and terrifying but civilians really did carry on as best they could. Dramatically, Churchill and the media recorded bold statements such as 'Let them all come' and 'We can take it'; these statements certainly caught the spirit of the time and were good for morale. Churchill and other dignitaries came to see the damage for themselves, walking down the blitzed streets and speaking to emergency service workers and local people. For many in the East End the visit that made the greatest impact upon them was that made by King George VI and Queen Elizabeth. Indeed, a bomb had fallen in the Palace quadrangle while they were in residence, blowing in many of the palace's windows and destroying the chapel. The King and Queen were filmed inspecting their bombed home, and the smiling Queen, stoical about the damage inflicted, thought first of her people and declared: 'I'm glad we have been bombed. It makes me feel I can look the East End in the face.'

Air Chief Marshal Sir Trafford Leigh Mallory, Commander of No. 12 Group RAF. (IWM CH 11943)

The opening day of the Blitz on 7 September also marked the first action of the newly created 'Big Wing', during which it claimed twenty-two victories

(although a comparison of actual German losses on the day indicates that a figure of about ten is more realistic). The theory of the Big Wing had been expounded by Trafford Leigh-Mallory, Air Officer Commanding 12 Group, and Squadron Leader Douglas Bader (Officer Commanding 242 Squadron), the idea being that more damage could be inflicted upon the enemy if they were attacked by three or more squadrons working together under one leader. Keith Park, AOC 11 Group, and many of his pilots were critical of the Big Wing because it took a long time to form up, whereas pilots in 12 Group countered that the 'Big Wing' could be airborne and assembled but their scramble orders often came too late. Either way, the Big Wing (later known as the 'Duxford Wing') certainly had a strong impact on the already diminished morale of the Luftwaffe pilots upon seeing such a force at a time when Göring was proclaiming RAF fighter command was depleted and very near complete destruction.

Squadron Leader Douglas Bader (fourth from right) and the pilots of No. 242 Squadron during the Battle of Britain.

In reality Fighter Command's reserves were dangerously low and it was beginning to struggle to maintain support for the losses suffered by 10, 11 and 12 Groups. The loss of a dozen squadron commanders and nearly forty more killed or wounded, left inexperienced junior officers and NCOs in at the deep end leading sections, flights and even a squadron. Acutely aware of the situation, Dowding introduced the Stabilisation Scheme on 8 September, whereby squadrons were regrouped by pilot experience, providing at least some relief for fatigued squadrons. Although the war in the air remained one that was bitterly fought, the turn of the Luftwaffe's focus from attacks upon airfields to the assault upon London, together with some patches of bad weather which prevented large-scale air assaults, gave the RAF valuable time to regroup.

Hitler and his commanders knew that time was running out; his invasion plans for early September had already been postponed to 11 September due to bad weather. Winter was not too far away, so the invasion was planned for 17 September and Göring sent out orders to all fighter and bomber bases to prepare for the pre-invasion assault to be carried out on England on Sunday 15 September.

Combat report submitted by Flight Lieutenant A. S. Forbes of No. 303 (Polish) Squadron RAF for action on 7 September 1940.

At 11:00 hrs over two hundred bombers and an unknown number of fighters were picked up on radar just off the coast near Calais, flying towards the English coast. At 11:05 the Spitfires of 72 and 92 Squadrons from Biggin Hill were the first to scramble, rapidly followed by the Hurricanes of 501 and 253. They were joined by more 11 Group Squadrons from Northolt, Kenley, Debden, Hendon, Martlesham, Hornchurch and Warmwell along with 609 Squadron from Middle Wallop in 10 Group. They were soon joined by the Duxford Wing, consisting of 19, 242, 302 and 310 Squadrons and 611 Squadron, flying from Digby.

The first fighters were approaching the southern coast of Kent as the Luftwaffe formations were a few miles off the coastline in a number of 'vic' (V-shaped) formations, making landfall at three main points: between Dover and Folkestone; near Ramsgate; and to the north of Dungeness, crossing over the cliffs in what Observers recalled looked like a giant herringbone. German intelligence had put RAF fighters down to as low as the last fifty. The young pilots of the RAF, though inexperienced, lacked no zeal and heroically set about the enemy.

The German formation made slow progress and the combat action was exceptionally heavy as the RAF fighters drew off their fighter escorts and gradually broke up their formation with a tenacious application of force. Luftwaffe Dornier 17 Front Gunner Hans Zonderlind recalled:

We saw the Hurricanes coming towards us and it seemed that the whole of the RAF was there, we had never seen so many British fighters coming at us at once. I saw a couple of our comrades go down, and we got hit once but it did no great damage. All around us were dogfights as the fighters went after each other, then as we were getting ready for our approach to the target, we saw what must have been a hundred RAF fighters coming at us. We thought that this must have been all the RAF planes were up at once, but where were they coming from, as we had been told that the RAF fighters were very close to extinction. We could not keep our present course, we turned to starboard and did all that we could to avoid the fighters and after a while I am sure we had lost our bearings, so we just dropped our bombs and made our retreat.

It was to be a hard-fought battle but it was one in which the Duxford Wing had time to form and worked to perfection. Indeed all the pilots of Fighter Command truly hammered home their attack, sending many bombers away riddled with bullets and trailing smoke; many simply dropped their bombs at random and fled. Those who pressed on to London managed to drop bombs on the south of the city with Lewisham, Lambeth and Camberwell suffering worst. During the raid, Sergeant Raymond Holmes of 504 Squadron took on three Dorniers at the same time; he was given the credit for bringing down the aircraft (Do 17 of 1/KG76) sent to bomb Buckingham Palace. The RAF fighters persisted in their harassment of the enemy and after about ten minutes the remaining Luftwaffe formation was smashed, with bombers flying at a variety of altitudes over an area about 15 miles wide and fleeing for the coast. Many of the Luftwaffe aircraft were badly damaged and did not make it back; a number of them crashed into the countryside or finally succumbed to damage over the English Channel and plunged into the waves.

There had been as many as two hundred combat actions and the figure of 185 German aircraft shot down on this single day was widely claimed in the press; the true figure revealed after the war was more like sixty, and the RAF had lost twenty-six. Irrespective of the true numbers, Luftwaffe aircrew were already in a low state of morale: many pilots were suffering from severe physical and mental strain, they had been severely criticised and blamed by their own High Command for the failure to achieve any notable successes, their intelligence had been proven woefully inaccurate again, and they had received another bloody nose from the RAF.

Historians have debated whether 15 September was the pivotal moment in the Battle of Britain. It certainly showed German High Command that air supremacy was not to be won easily, nor in a brief space of time, and went a long way to convince them that it might not be won at all. The threat of imminent invasion rapidly began to fade and Hitler shelved his immediate plans for invasion on 19 September, ordering his invasion fleet of barges and troops to be dispersed. For the airmen and for

Pattern of condensation trails left by British and German aircraft after a dogfight, 18 September 1940. (IWM H 4219)

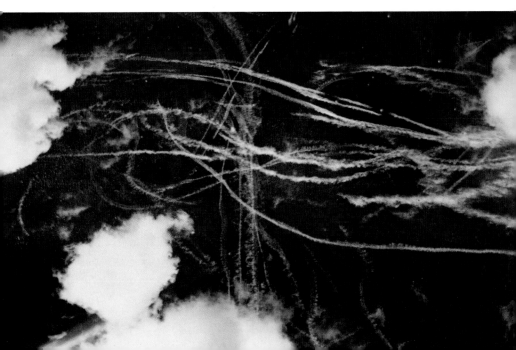

the British people as a whole the achievements of 15 September provided a massive boost to morale when it was most needed. The heroic actions and achievements of the plucky RAF fighter pilots who flew 'gainst odds uncounted', as reported across the media of the day, stirred up emotions akin to those aroused by the 'epic of Dunkirk', except this time it was a victory; 15 September is still marked as Battle of Britain Day. There was still more fighting to be done, as the Battle raged on for several more weeks, but German tactics were changing and the last major daylight raid on London was conducted on 30 September.

PHASE 5: 3 OCTOBER TO 31 OCTOBER

The Luftwaffe primarily concentrated its bombing raids upon London, predominantly at night; its second imperative was to attack the arms factories of the West Midlands, again chiefly by night; and thirdly it aimed to disrupt war production plants and factories at a variety of locations across Britain, using fighter-bombers in daylight raids. According to German sources 9,000 tons of bombs were dropped on Britain during October 1940. Among the cities to suffer were Birmingham, Bristol, Coventry, Liverpool, Manchester, Hull, Southampton and Glasgow. The Italian Air Force also flew into active airspace in this last phase of the Battle, flying a sortie towards Kent, but turned away having been discouraged by anti-aircraft fire.

The last big clash took place on 29 October when fighters from 602 and 222 Squadrons attacked a group of Messerschmitt Bf 109s during bombing raids on London and Southampton. Members of 602 Squadron claimed eight enemy fighters for no loss, and the total losses for the day were nineteen Luftwaffe to

A news vendor casts his eyes to the sky during the Battle. (IWM HU 810)

seven RAF. During the month of October the Luftwaffe lost a total of 325 aircraft and the RAF 128. The RAF lost one hundred pilots and a further eighty-five were wounded.

The skies over Britain remained a dangerous place. Many fighter pilots who had served in the Battle of Britain were to recall, with bitter regret, that the air battles of October 1940 were in many ways more dangerous than those that preceded them. The Messerschmitt Bf 109s took to flying at higher altitudes, often above 25,000 feet, and had the advantage as the RAF fighters found themselves climbing through hazy autumn sunshine and cloud to reach them. Tragically, many of those who had served through the most dramatic months of the Battle were now lost in the aftermath of victory.

From the German point of view, they were still fighting the Battle of Britain. They had simply changed their tactics and the air raids of the Blitz continued until May 1941, when Hitler concentrated his efforts on the Eastern Front and required his bombers in preparation for the invasion of Russia. The Blitz on London had destroyed or damaged more than a million houses, and more than twenty thousand civilians had been killed by bombing in London alone. The Battle of Britain was over, but more bombing campaigns were to come, and there would be many more air raids on London and across Britain before the end of the war.

Blackout times were published in the daily newspapers.

A group of pilots of No. 303 (Polish) Squadron, Royal Air Force at Northolt, October 1940. (IWM H 001535)

ANTI-AIRCRAFT
UNITS OF THE
TERRITORIAL
ARMY

AND MAKE BRITAIN
A STRONGHOLD OF FREEDOM

Lance Cattermole
1938

ON THE GROUND

IT MAY seem incredible now but during the Battle of Britain a popular family activity was to go into the country, especially across the beautiful rolling countryside of the 'Garden of England' in Kent around the Biggin Hill area, with a flask and picnic to sit and watch the dog fights above them, in much the same way as families would go to see an air show today. Some even made quite a habit of the event and got wise to selecting spots near ditches or trees where they could dive for cover from stray bullets and wreckage.

From May and June 1940 the British people really did feel they were on a war footing and that their services would be needed. In typically British style, people of all ages wanted to do something for the war effort by joining any one (or more) of the voluntary services on the Home Front, and continued to do this work through the darkest days of the Blitz. The 'carry on' spirit is all the more remarkable when it is recalled that so many people, after a day at work, would frequently report for duty at a host of wartime organisations as diverse as the Home Guard (training to stand ready in the event of invasion), serving as a Special or War Reserve Constable, volunteering for ARP work (with such duties as Air Raid Warden or rescue worker – some of them on the front line of the Blitz), or the Women's Voluntary Service (running the rest centres for those who had been bombed out of their homes or workers who had to stop for sustenance). Others joined The British Red Cross Society or St John Ambulance Brigade – many of their number were female ambulance drivers who bravely drove through the stricken streets to pick up casualties and remove them to hospital – or one of the multitude of organisations running canteens and of course helping out the brave men of the National Fire Service and Auxiliary Fire Service. Many of these volunteers modestly recalled that they had preferred to join such organisations rather than spend another uncomfortable night in an air-raid shelter.

The ground defences during the Battle of Britain relied on five key factors: radar, anti-aircraft artillery, searchlights, barrage balloons and the Observer Corps. In 1940 a chain of twenty-nine Radio Direction Finding (RDF) or

Opposite:
A late-1930s recruiting poster for anti-aircraft units of the Territorial Army.

Chain Home: AMES Type 1 CH East Coast radar installation at Poling, Sussex. (IWM CH 15173)

radar stations along the south and east coasts of England (with a few further inland such as Stoke Holy Cross in Norfolk and Ottercops Moss in Northumberland) provided a long-distance early warning system for the RAF. Enemy intruders flying at 10,000 feet could be detected at ranges of 50 to 120 miles. A further string of Chain Home Low stations, for the detection of aircraft flying at low altitudes below the current radar, was built during the

Air defences depicted on Wills's Cigarette cards.

WILLS'S CIGARETTES

WILLS'S CIGARETTES

WILLS'S CIGARETTES

ANTI-AIRCRAFT SEARCHLIGHT

ANTI-AIRCRAFT SEARCHLIGHT. The duty of anti-aircraft searchlight units is to find and illuminate enemy aircraft so that they can be attacked by our own fighter machines or fired at by anti-aircraft guns. The searchlight has a glass paraboloid reflector 36 in. in diameter and an electric arc lamp which gives a light of many millions of candle power. In fine weather the searchlight has a range of over 5 miles. The complete searchlight detachment consists of 10 men who work the searchlight, a sound locator (illustrated and described on Card No. 48) and a generating plant which provides the necessary power for the arc lamp. (No. 47)

REPRESENTATION OF BALLOON BARRAGE FOR DEFENCE OF LONDON

ANTI-AIRCRAFT SOUND LOCATOR

REPRESENTATION OF BALLOON BARRAGE FOR DEFENCE OF LONDON. The balloon barrage forms an important part of the co-ordinated scheme—consisting of guns, searchlights, fighter aeroplanes and balloons—for the air defence of London. In time of war, the balloons would be disposed in a rough circle round the perimeter of London. Each balloon is attached by a steel cable to a winch on the ground by which it can be let up or hauled down to the required height. The balloon cables form a "death trap" to any enemy aeroplane colliding with them. The balloons are organized in flights and squadrons, the squadrons being on an auxiliary basis manned by volunteers with a small nucleus of fully trained regular personnel. (No. 46)

ARP

ANTI-AIRCRAFT SOUND LOCATOR. One sound locator is an essential part of the equipment of an Anti-Aircraft Searchlight Detachment and is used for directing the searchlight beam on to a target which can only be heard. It is manned by a crew of 3. Two of these are listening numbers, one uses the pair of trumpets which gives the horizontal direction of the target, the other uses the pair which gives the vertical direction. The third member of the crew uses the sight which makes an allowance for the speed of the target; this member telephones instructions to the searchlight controller, who then moves the searchlight beam so that the target is illuminated. Large numbers of these sound locators are used in the Air Defence of Great Britain. (No. 48)

war. Although the Luftwaffe deliberately targeted the radar stations they never fully understood their crucial role in 1940 and were continually frustrated at the speed with which these bases appeared to return to operational service after suffering an attack.

The 'Roof over Britain' was provided by Anti-Aircraft Command. Formed as late as April 1939, anti-aircraft forces were integrated with Fighter Command and overall operational control was with Dowding, who maintained an excellent working relationship with the head of AA Command, Lieutenant General Sir Frederick Pile. The problem was that AA Command had only received a third of the light and half of the heavy anti-aircraft guns they required by July 1940. Fortunately the searchlights that operated with the artillery defences were more plentiful, and performed a valuable service locating enemy aircraft in darkness while their crew often took on the function of a listening and/or spotting post in daylight hours, reporting any enemy intruders to the gun Operations Rooms. Despite the shortage of guns, AA Command did a sterling job at batteries and emplacements protecting aircraft factories, airfields, industrial areas, naval

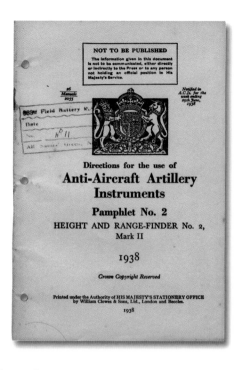

Pre-war training manual for anti-aircraft artillery instruments.

40 mm Bofors gun and crew at Stanmore in Middlesex, 28 June 1940. (IWM H 1967)

43

bases, ports and at strategic points around the coast and brought down about three hundred enemy aircraft during the Battle of Britain.

RAF Balloon Command had been established in 1938 to operate barrage balloons over vulnerable targets such as cities, factory complexes and ports, providing simple and effective protection from enemy aircraft (especially dive bombers) and causing enemy bombers to fly higher, thus reducing bombing accuracy. By late July 1940 there were 1,466 barrage balloons in service, 450 of which were deployed in the defence of London.

The RAF airfields themselves were defended by light anti-aircraft defences, the responsibility of the Royal Artillery. Bofors guns were commonly used, supported by RAF gunners with light machine guns such as the Bren on ground mounts. The necessity for such airfield defences within the RAF was soon recognised: a new trade of Ground Gunner was created in the autumn of 1940 and the RAF Regiment was formed in 1942.

The RAF's air-raid reporting and fighter control system was vital to Fighter Command's success in the Battle of Britain. Although in its infancy during the Battle, this system provided all levels of command with an up-to-date and continuous picture of what was happening during an enemy raid,

Staff of 12 Sector Operations Room at Duxford. The call signs of fighter squadrons controlled by this Sector can be seen on the wall behind the operator sitting third from left. The Controller is sitting fifth from the left, and next to him is the Army Liaison Officer. (IWM CH 1401)

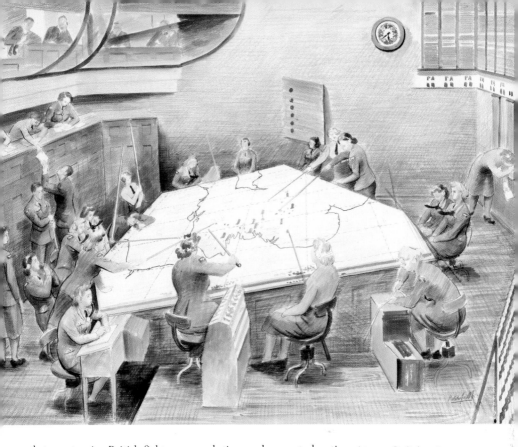

and strove to give British fighters enough time and accurate locations to intercept the enemy, allowing Dowding to use his limited resources of pilots and aircraft to the best possible advantage.

An RAF Fighter Station's Operations Room staff would consist of both regular RAF and Volunteer Reserves, Army personnel and members of the Women's Auxiliary Air Force. The Operations Room would be commanded by an RAF Officer known as the Controller, whose role was to deploy the fighter aircraft to the best possible positions to engage the enemy and to keep in contact with the pilots via radio telephone. He would be supported by Ops A, an airman who would receive action messages from Group HQ, and Ops B, who was responsible for communications to the airfield and its satellites. It was also the responsibility of Ops B to update the status information of the squadrons in the Group (such as 'ordered to readiness', 'at standby', or 'left ground') displayed on the tote board in the room, and liaise with other RAF units. There would also be an army officer, assisted by two army signallers, who would liaise between the AA defences and the RAF. Meanwhile the WAAFs would be situated around the large map table, wearing headsets through which they would receive reports of enemy raids from the

Radiolocation plotters at 11 Group Headquarters, Uxbridge, by Roland Vivian Pitchforth RA. (IWM ART LD 2320)

Above: Observer Corps lapel badge, often seen worn on the berets of members.

Above right: Early Observer Corps arm band worn when on duty.

Observer Corps and RDF (RADAR) stations (via the Filter Room at Fighter Command HQ). They would then plot the information onto the map table along with the positions of friendly aircraft, providing the Controller with a continuous picture of the situation in the air.

One service, however, directly contributed to the efforts of the RAF during the Battle of Britain more than any other: the thirty thousand civilian volunteers of the Observer Corps. The British Chain Home radar defence system was only capable of giving warning of enemy aircraft approaching the British coast; once these aircraft were above the mainland the only means of tracking their position was by visual plotting, the duty performed by the Observer Corps. Begun in the 1920s, the OC had grown and developed throughout the 1930s. The first observation posts consisted of little more than wooden sheds or lean-tos reinforced by sandbags, which were eventually replaced by more substantial brick-built structures, also protected by sandbags. Constructed by the OC personnel themselves, no two observation posts were alike. Their locations were also varied, from playing fields to farm land, on hill and cliff tops and, in urban areas, on the roofs of public buildings and factories. Each observation post would be between 6 and 12 miles from its neighbour, its precise location governed by its proximity to telephone lines. Observation posts were organised into groups of thirty to forty, controlled from one of the forty Observer Corps Centres situated across the country.

Certificate No. 11634

FORM 693.

Air Defence of Great Britain

This is to certify that

G. B. Parnell

is qualified as a member of the Observer Corps of Special Constables.

A.D. Warrington-Morris

Head Quarters, Observer Corps,
Stanmore, Middlesex.

Commandant,
Observer Corps.

Date 17th May 1939

(2447-204) Wt. 9126—28 5,000 4/39 T.S. 700

Opposite bottom:
Membership
certificate for the
Observer Corps.

Left: A Battle
of Britain
Observer
Corps post.
(IWM CH 2477)

Some observers were issued with high-quality Royal Navy binoculars but most provided their own; the main instrument they were trained upon and issued with was the Micklethwait height adjuster, which (although a rather Heath Robinson arrangement by all accounts) was cheap to produce and simple to operate. One observer would sight aircraft along a piece of wood while another worked a height bar and read off height and direction. The bar was mechanically connected to a vertical pointer, which would plot the approximate

Aircraft
identification
manual, 1940.

47

position of the aircraft on the circular map grid. Observers would then report the map co-ordinates, height, time, Sector Clock code-colour and number of aircraft for each sighting to the aircraft plotters at the Observer Corps Centre. (Sector Clocks have red, yellow and blue segments that represent time lapses, enabling the age of a plot to be deduced by its colour.) Here the plotters, wearing telephone headsets, maintained constant communication with their

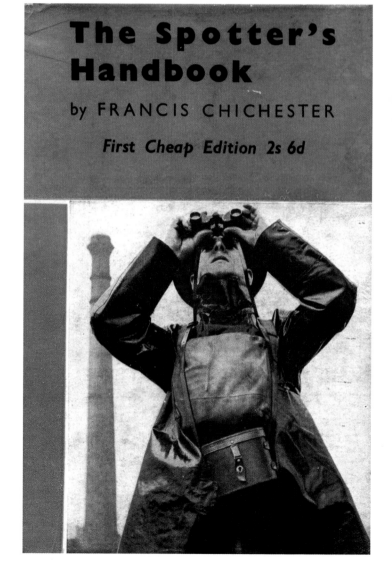

The Spotter's Handbook by Francis Chichester (1941).

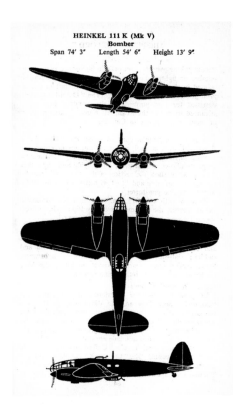

HEINKEL 111 K (Mk V)
Bomber
Span 74' 3"   Length 54' 6"   Height 13' 9"

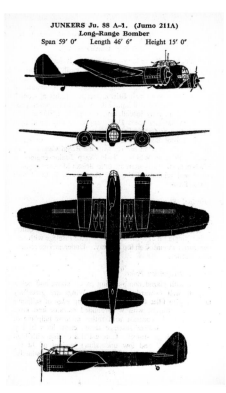

JUNKERS Ju. 88 A–1. (Jumo 211A)
Long–Range Bomber
Span 59' 0"   Length 46' 6"   Height 15' 0"

allocated posts (usually three in number) and would transpose the information sent to them onto the main plotting table map upon which the various reports could be compiled, the positions of the aircraft marked and their progress observed. Information would then be passed by 'tellers' to the relevant neighbouring OC centres, searchlight units, anti-aircraft batteries, and to its Sector Control, thence to Fighter Command via Group Headquarters. This efficient system made it possible to get fighter aircraft into the air and intercept within five minutes, and allowed timely air-raid warnings to be given.

Aircraft identification silhouettes featured in books, on posters and cards – standard training aids for Observers.

During the Battle of Britain the OC operated twenty-four hours a day, seven days a week, plotting enemy aircraft and passing this essential information through the command chain. OC personnel were deployed in two specific roles: Class A were required to undertake fifty-six hours' duty per week; Class B personnel reported for up to twenty-four hours' duty per week.

In recognition of the role it played during the Battle of Britain the OC was granted the title Royal Observer Corps in April 1941 by King George VI. The ROC then became a uniformed civil defence organisation administered by RAF Fighter Command.

NEVER IN THE FIELD
OF HUMAN CONFLICT...

THE FAMOUS TERM 'THE FEW' was originated in the speech by Prime Minister Winston Churchill during the height of the Battle of Britain on 20 August 1940, in which he stated:

> The gratitude of every home in our Island, in our Empire, and indeed throughout the world, except in the abodes of the guilty, goes out to the British airmen who, undaunted by odds, unwearied in their constant challenge and mortal danger, are turning the tide of the World War by their prowess and by their devotion. Never in the field of human conflict was so much owed by so many to so few.

'The few' were the 2,937 pilots and other aircrew from Great Britain and from overseas, who were officially recognised as having taken part in the

Opposite: The famous 'Few' poster, produced in 1940. (IWM PST 14972)

Left: RAF badge on the headstone of a Battle of Britain pilot.

Battle of Britain with the award of the Battle of Britain clasp. This was given for having flown at least one authorised operational sortie with an eligible unit of RAF Fighter Command between 10 July and 31 October 1940. A total of 422 of these men were wounded, and 544 lost their lives during the Battle of Britain. Many pilots came from overseas, fought and died while serving in Fighter Command and the Fleet Air Arm during the Battle:

Nationality	Number Served	Number Killed
Poland	145	30
New Zealand	126	13
Canada	98	20
Czechoslovakia	88	7
Australia	33	14
Belgium	29	6
South Africa	25	9
France	13	–
United States	11	1
Ireland	10	–
Rhodesia	3	–
Jamaica	1	–
Newfoundland	1	–
Palestine	1	–
Barbados	1	–

The first Battle of Britain Day was commemorated on Sunday 15 September 1944 and has usually been observed on the third Sunday of every

The remarkable DFC, DFM and Bar group of medals awarded to Battle of Britain pilot Flight Lieutenant Geoffrey 'Sammy' Allard. Tragically, he was killed in a flying accident on 13 March 1941.

Air Chief Marshal Lord Dowding talking with Group Captain D. R. S. Bader and other veteran fighter pilots before they took off from North Weald, Essex, for the Battle of Britain Anniversary fly-past over London on 15 September 1945. (IWM CH 16283)

September ever since; the event is still marked by special events across the country, as well as street collections that have raised millions of pounds for the Royal Air Force Association Wings Appeal. A national memorial to 'The Few' was erected in 1993 by The Battle of Britain Memorial Trust at Capel le Ferne, on the white cliffs between Dover and Kent. The Battle of Britain London Monument, instigated by The Battle of Britain Historical Society, was unveiled in September 2005, while the RAF's Battle of Britain

The first four Polish recipients of the Distinguished Flying Cross, No. 303 (Polish) Squadron RAF, wearing their awards after a presentation ceremony by Air Marshal W. Sholto-Douglas at Leconfield, Yorkshire, December 1940. Left to right: Flying Officer Witold Urbanowicz, Pilot Officer Jan Zumbach, Pilot Officer Mirosław Feri and Flying Officer Zdzisław Henneberg. (IWM CH 1840)

Above: The wartime HMSO booklet that told the story of the Battle of Britain.

Memorial Flight has continued to provide an airborne tribute since it was formally established in 1959.

The legacy of the Battle of Britain, and its impact upon the course of the war and morale during the conflict, is inestimable. Those who contributed to that victory, such as the members of the Air Transport Auxiliary (one in eight of whose pilots were women) who delivered aircraft to RAF stations across the country, the countless men and women war workers who worked night and day to build the aircraft and turn out munitions, the WAAFs who bravely carried on as drivers, clerks, telephonists, cooks and orderlies on the fighter stations despite facing daily attacks, and the thousands of male and female civilians who 'did their bit' as volunteers for Home Front services through the darkest days and nights of The Battle of Britain should not be forgotten.

Sergeant Joan E. Mortimer, Flight Officer Elspeth C. Henderson and Sergeant Helen E. Turner, recipients of the Military Medal for gallantry, standing outside damaged buildings at Biggin Hill, Kent. All three were WAAF teleprinter operators who stayed at their posts and continued to work the defence lines during the heavy Luftwaffe attacks on Biggin Hill on 1 September 1940. (IWM CH 1550)

FURTHER READING

Bickers, R.T. *The Battle of Britain*. Salamander, London, 1990.

Brickhill, P. *Reach for the Sky*. Collins, London, 1954.

Bungay, S. *The Most Dangerous Enemy: A History of the Battle of Britain*. Aurum Press, London, 2001.

Barker, R. *That Eternal Summer*. Collins, London, 1990.

Bushby, J. *Air Defence of Great Britain*. Ian Allen, London, 1973.

Dunn, B. N. *Big Wing: The Biography of Air Chief Marshal Sir Trafford Leigh-Mallory*. Airlife Publishing, Shrewsbury, 1992.

Escott, B. E. *The WAAF: A History of the Women's Auxiliary Air Force in the Second World War*. Shire Publications, Oxford, 2001.

Falconer, J. *Life as a Battle of Britain Pilot* (2010) The History Press, Stroud, Gloucestershire

Flint, P. *Dowding and Headquarters Fighter Command*. Airlife Publishing, Shrewsbury, 1996.

Franks, N. *Battle of Britain*. Bison Books, London, 1981.

Galland, A. *The Luftwaffe Fighter Force, the View from the Cockpit*. Greenhill Books, Barnsley, 1998.

Holmes, T. *Spitfire vs Bf 109: Battle of Britain*. Osprey Publishing, Oxford, 2007.

Jefford, Wing Commander C.G. *RAF Squadrons*. Airlife, Shrewsbury, 2001.

Kent, J. *One of the Few: A Triumphant Story of Combat in the Battle of Britain*. The History Press, Stroud, 2008.

Kingcome, B. *A Willingness to Die: Memories from Fighter Command*. The History Press, Stroud, 2006.

Korda, M. *With Wings Like Eagles: The Untold Story of the Battle of Britain*. JR Books, London, 2010.

Longmate, N. *Island Fortress: The Defence of Britain 1603–1945*. Grafton, London, 1993.

Mason, F. *Battle Over Britain*. McWhirter Twins Ltd., 1969.

Orange, V. *Park: The Biography of Air Chief Marshall Sir Keith Park*. Grub Street, London, 2001.

Pile, Sir F. *Ack-Ack: Britain's Defence Against Air Attack in the Second World War*. Harrap, London, 1949.

Price, A. *Battle of Britain: The Hardest Day 18 August 1940*. Harper Collins, London, 1980.

Price, A. *Battle of Britain Day: 15 September 1940*. Greenhill Books, London, 1999.

Ramsey, W.G. (ed.) *The Battle of Britain Then and Now*. After the Battle, 1980.

Ramsey, W.G. (ed.) *The Blitz Then and Now*. (three vols from 1988) After the Battle.

Simpson, G. *A Dictionary of the Battle of Britain*. Halsgrove, Wellington, Somerset, 2009.

Steinhilper, U. *Spitfire on My Tail: A View from the Other Side*. Independent Books, Bromley, 2009.

Walker, O. *Sailor Malan*. Cassell, London, 1953.

Ward, A. *A Nation Alone: The Battle of Britain – 1940*. Osprey, Oxford.

Wood, D. *Target England*. (1980) Jane's, London, 1980.

Wood, D. *Attack Warning Red: History of the Royal Observer Corps*. Jane's, London, 1976.

Wynn, K.G. *Men of the Battle of Britain*. Gliddon Books, Norwich, 1989.

INDEX